INSTRUCTIONS

FOR

SERJEANT-INSTRUCTORS OF MILITIA, YEOMANRY, AND VOLUNTEERS

IN REGARD TO

THE CARE, INSPECTION, &c.,

OF

MARTINI-HENRY, MARTINI-METFORD, AND MARTINI-ENFIELD ARMS.

WAR OFFICE, 1896.

The Naval & Military Press Ltd
© 2008

In reprinting in facsimile from the original, any imperfections are inevitably reproduced and the quality may fall short of modern type and cartographic standards.

INDEX.

	PAGE
Nomenclature of parts	3
Directions for cleaning	12
Directions with regard to the periodical inspection of arms by Serjeant-Instructors	13
Directions for stripping and assembling the arm and action	14
Examination of strikers	18
Easing springs	18
Instructions for replacing strikers and mainsprings in the field	19
Instructions for using trigger-testers	19
Names of component parts of the Martini-Henry, Martini-Metford, and Martini-Enfield action which can be replaced by the Serjeant-Instructors	20
Proportions of spare parts for repairs	21
Tools required	21

PLATES.

I. Martini-Henry carbines.

II. Martini-Henry rifle (Mark II).

III. Martini-Henry rifle (Mark III).

IV. Martini-Metford carbines, special components.

INSTRUCTIONS FOR THE CARE, INSPECTION, CLEANING, &c., OF MARTINI-HENRY, MARTINI-METFORD, AND MARTINI-ENFIELD ARMS.

(*See* Plates I., II., III., and IV.)

1. The following table shows the parts which are interchangeable, or otherwise, between the rifles, M.-H., Marks II and III, and rifle, M.-E., Mark I; carbines, Artillery, M.-H., Marks I, II, and III; carbine, Cavalry, M.-H., Mark I; carbines, Artillery, M.-M., Marks II and III; and carbines, Cavalry, M.-M., Marks I,* II,* and III :—

Nomenclature of Parts.	
Band, lower, rifle, M.-H., Mark II	Interchangeable between Marks II and III, M.-H., also Marks II and III, M.-H. Artillery carbines.
Band, lower, rifle, M.-E., Mark I	Special.
Band, lower, carbine, Cavalry, M.-H., Mark I	Interchangeable between Mark I, Cavalry, M.-H., Mark I, Artillery, M.-H., Mark I* and II*, Cavalry carbines, M.-M.
Band, lower, screw	Interchangeable between all M.-H. and M.-M. arms that have lower bands.
", ", ", rifle, M.-E., Mark I	Special.
Band, lower, stop-pin	Interchangeable between all arms that have lower bands stop-pins.
* ", upper, rifle, M.-H., Mark II	Interchangeable between Marks II and III, M.-H., rifles, also Marks II and III, M.-H. Artillery carbines.
‡ Band, upper, rifle, M.-E., Mark I	Special.
†Band, upper, carbine, Cavalry, M.-H., Mark I	Interchangeable between Mark I, Cavalry, M.-H., and Mark I*, M.-M. carbine, Cavalry.

* Same, but slightly altered for Marks II and III, M.-H. Artillery carbines.
† Same, but slightly altered for Mark I*, M.-M. Cavalry carbines.
‡ This is a M.-H. rifle, Mark III, band altered.

Nomenclature of Parts.	
Band, upper, carbine, Cavalry, M.-M., Mark II*	Special.
Band, upper, carbine, Artillery, M.-H., Mark I	,,
Band, upper, carbine, Artillery, M.-M., Marks II and III, and Cavalry, M.-M., Mark III	In these carbines the upper band is combined with the nose-cap.
Band, upper, screw, M.-H. rifle, Mark II	Interchangeable between Marks II and III, M.-H., and Mark I, M.-E. rifles, also Marks I, II, and III, M.-H. Artillery carbines.
Band, upper, screw, carbine, Cavalry, M.-H., Mark I	Interchangeable between Mark I, M.-H. Cavalry, and Mark I*, M.-M. carbine, Cavalry.
Band, upper, screw, carbine, Cavalry, M.-M., Mark II	Special.
Band, upper, screw nut, M.-H. rifle, Mark II	Interchangeable between Marks II and III, M.-H., and Mark I, M.-E. rifles; also Marks I, II, and III, Artillery carbines, M.-H.
†Band, swivel, screw, Artillery carbine, M.-M., Mark II	Interchangeable between Marks II and III, Artillery carbines, M.-M.
Band, upper, stop-pin, rifle, M.-H., Mark II	Interchangeable between Marks II and III, M.-H., and Mark I M.-E. rifles; also Marks II and III, M.-H. Artillery carbine.
Barrel, with body, rifle, M.-H., Mark II	Special.
Barrel, with body, rifle, M.-H., Mark III	,,
Barrel, with body, M.-E. rifle, Mark I	,,
Barrel, with body, carbine, M.-H., Cavalry, Mark I	Interchangeable between Marks I and III, M.-H. Artillery, and Mark I, M.-H. carbines, Cavalry.
Barrel, with body, Artillery, carbine, M.-H., Mark II	Special.

---

* In some carbines, the upper band screw has been reduced in the middle to clear clearing rod.

† In carbines, Cavalry, M.-M., Mark III, and Artillery, M.-M., Marks II and III, the nose-cap is combined with upper band.

Nomenclature of Parts.	
Barrel, with body, Cavalry, carbine, M.-M., Mark I*	Interchangeable between Marks I* and II*, M.M. carbines, Cavalry.
Barrel, with body, Cavalry, carbine, M.-M., Mark III	Special.
Barrel, with body, Artillery, carbine, M.-M., Mark II	,,
Barrel, with body, Artillery, carbine, M.-M., Mark III	,,
Barrel, stud-pin, rifle, M.-H., Mark II	Interchangeable between Mark II, M.-H., rifle, and Mark II, M.-H. Artillery carbines.
*Barrel, stud-pin, Cavalry, carbine, M.-M., Mark III	Interchangeable between Mark III, M.-M., Cavalry, and Mark II, M.-M., Artillery carbines.
Blocks, breech, rifle, M.-H., Mark II	Interchangeable between Mark II, M.-H. rifle, and Mark II, M.-H. Artillery carbines.
Blocks, breech, rifle, M.-H., Mark III	Interchangeable between Mark III, M.-H. rifle, and Marks I and III, M.-H., Artillery, and Mark I, M.-H. Cavalry carbines.
†Blocks, breech, rifle, M.-E., Mark I	Special.
Blocks, breech, M.-M.	Interchangeable between Marks I*, II*, and III, M.-M. Cavalry, and Marks II, and III, M.-M. Artillery carbines.
Block, axis-pin	Interchangeable between all arms.
Butt plate	,, ,, ,,
,, ,, screws (2)	,, ,, ,,
Cover, leather, back-sight, Cavalry, carbine, M.-H., Mark I	Interchangeable between Mark I, M.-H., and Marks I* and II*, M.-M. Cavalry carbines.
Cover, leather, back-sight, Cavalry, carbine, M.-M., Mark III	Special.
Cover, leather, back-sight, screws (1 long, 1 short)	Interchangeable between all Cavalry carbines.
Disc, marking, butt	Interchangeable between Mark I, M.-E. rifle; Marks II and III, M.-H. Artillery, Mark III, M.-M. Cavalry, and Marks II and III, M.-M. Artillery carbines.
,, ,, screw	Ditto.

* Same pin as in M.-H. Mark II rifle, but altered in length.
† Issued assembled with face plate and screw.

Nomenclature of Parts.	
Extractor, M.-H., Mark III	Interchangeable between Marks II and III, M.-H. rifles; Mark I, M.-H. Cavalry, and Marks I, II, and III, M.-H. Artillery carbines.
,, M.-M.	Interchangeable between Marks I*, II*. and III, M.-M. Cavalry, and Marks II. and III, M.-M. Artillery carbines.
,, M.-E., Mark I	Special.
,, axis-pin	Interchangeable between all arms.
‡Face plate block, rifle, M.-E., Mark I	Special.
‡Face plate block, screw, rifle M.E., Mark I	,,
Guard	Interchangeable between all arms.
,, swivel	,, ,, Marks II and III, M.-H. rifles.
,, ,, screw	Ditto.
Hook, fore-end M.-H.	Interchangeable between Mark III, M.-H., and Mark I, M.-E. rifles; Mark I, M.-H. Cavalry, Marks I and III, M.-H. Artillery, and Mark III, M.-M. Artillery carbines.
* ,, ,, M.-M.	Interchangeable between Marks I* and II*, M.-M. Cavalry carbines.
,, ,, screws (2)	Interchangeable between all arms having fore-end hooks.
Indicator	Interchangeable between all arms.
Lever rifle, M.H., Mark II	,, ,, Marks II and III, M.-H., and Mark I, M.E. rifles, and all M.H. and M.M. carbines.
,, catch-block ,,	Same as lever.
,, ,, ,, pin	Interchangeable between all arms.
,, ,, ,, spring	,, ,, ,,
Mainspring, M.-H.	,, ,, M.-H. arms.
,, M.-M.	,, ,, M.-M. and M.E. arms.
†Nose-cap, rifle, M.-H., Mark II	,, ,, Marks II and III, M.-H., and Mark I, M.-E. rifles.
Nose-cap, carbine, Cavalry, M.-H., Mark I	Special.

* With rod nut brazed on.
† The same but slightly altered in M.E. rifle Mark I.
‡ Not supplied as spare parts.

Nomenclature of Parts.	
Nose-cap, carbine, Artillery, M.-H., Mark I	Special.
*Nose-cap, carbine, Artillery, M.-H., Mark II	Interchangeable between Marks II and III, M.-H. Artillery carbines.
†Nose-cap, carbine, Cavalry, M.-M., Mark I*	Special.
‡Nose-cap, carbine, Cavalry, M.-M., Mark II*	,,
§Nose-cap, carbine, Cavalry, M.-M., Mark III	,,
§Nose-cap, carbine, Artillery, M.-M., Mark II	Interchangeable between Marks II and III, M.-M. Artillery carbines.
Nose-cap, screw, rifle, M.-H., Mark II (short)	Interchangeable between Marks II and III, M.-H. rifles, and Marks II and III, M.-H. Artillery carbines.
Nose-cap, screw, carbine, Artillery, M.-M., Mark II	Interchangeable between Marks II and III, M.-M. Artillery carbines.
Nose-cap, screw, carbine, Cavalry, M.-H., Mark I (2)	Interchangeable between Mark I, M.-H., Marks I* and II*, M.-M., Cavalry, and Mark I, M.-H. Artillery carbines.
Nose-cap, screw, carbine, Cavalry, M.-M., Mark III	Special.
Rod, cleaning, rifle, M.-H., Mark II	Interchangeable between Marks II and III, M.-H. rifles.
Rod, cleaning, carbine, M.-H.	Special in all four M.-H. carbines.
Rod, clearing, rifle, M.-E., Mark I	Special.
Rod, clearing, carbine, Cavalry, M.-M., Mark I*	Interchangeable between Marks I* and II*, M.-M. Cavalry carbines.
Rod, clearing, carbine, Cavalry, M.-M., Mark III	Interchangeable between Mark III, M.-M., and Marks II and III, M.-M. Artillery carbines.
‖Rod-holder, rifle, M.-H., Mark II	Interchangeable between Marks II and III, M.-H., and Mark I, M.-E. rifles; also Marks II and III, M.-H. Artillery, carbines.

* This is a M.-H. rifle, Mark II, nose-cap, altered.
† This is a M.-H. carbine, Cavalry, Mark I, nose-cap altered.
‡ This is a M.-H. carbine, Artillery, Mark I, nose-cap altered.
§ In carbines, Cavalry, M.-M. Mark III, and Artillery, M.-M. Marks II and III, the nose-cap is combined with upper band.
‖ The nose-cap acts as rod-holder in M.-H. carbine, Artillery, and Cavalry, Mark I.

Nomenclature of Parts.	
Rod-holder, screws, rifle, M.-H., Mark II (2) (1 long and 1 short)	Interchangeable between Marks II and III, M.-H., and Mark I, M.-E. rifles; also Marks II and III, M.-H. Artillery carbines.
Rod-nut, rifle, M.-E., Mark I	Special.
Rod-nut, carbine, Cavalry, M.-M., Mark III	Interchangeable between Mark III. Cavalry, and Marks II and III, M.-M. Artillery carbines.
Screw, keeper, indicator	Interchangeable between all arms.
,, ,, stop-nut	,, ,, ,,
†Stock, butt, rifle, M.-H., Mark II	,, ,, ,,
Stock, bolt, rifle, M.-H., Mark II	,, ,, ,,
Stock, bolt, washer, rifle, M.-H., Mark II	,, ,, ,,
Stock, fore-end, rifle, M.-H., Mark II	Special.
Stock, fore-end, rifle, M.-H., Mark III	,,
Stock, fore-end, rifle, M.-E., Mark I	Special, converted from stock, fore-end, rifle, M.-H., Mark III
Stock, fore-end, carbine, Cavalry, M.-H., Mark I	Special.
Stock, fore-end, Artillery, carbine, M.-H., Mark I	,,
Stock, fore-end, Artillery, carbine, M.-H., Mark II	Special, converted from stock, fore-end, M.-H., Mark II, rifle
Stock, fore-end, Artillery, carbine, M.-H., Mark III	Special.
Stock, fore-end, carbine, Cavalry, M.-M., Mark I*	Special, converted from stock, fore-end, M.-H., carbine, Cavalry, Mark I.
Stock, fore-end, carbine, Cavalry, M.-M., Mark II*	Special, converted from stock, fore-end, M.-H. Artillery carbines, Mark I.
Stock, fore-end, carbine, Cavalry, M.-M., Mark III	Special.
Stock, fore-end, Artillery, carbine. M.-M., Mark II	,,

† Stocks, butt, for Marks II and III, M.-H., Artillery, Mark III, M.-M., Cavalry, and Marks II and III, M.-M. Artillery carbines, and Mark I, M.-E. rifles, have a marking disc recessed in the butt-end, on the right side.

Nomenclature of Parts.	
Stock, fore-end, Artillery, carbine, M.-M., Mark III	Special.
Sight, back, rifle, M.-H., Mark II	,,
Sight, back, rifle, M.-H., Mark III	,,
Sight, back, rifle, M.-E., Mark I	,,
Sight, back, carbine, Cavalry, M.-H., Mark I	Interchangeable between Mark I, M.-H., Cavalry, and Marks I and III, M.-H., Artillery carbines.
Sight, back, carbine, Cavalry, M.-M., Mark I*	Interchangeable between Marks I* and II,* M.-M. Cavalry carbines.
Sight, back, carbine, Cavalry, M.-M., Mark III	Interchangeable between Mark III, M.-M., Cavalry, and Marks II and III, M.-M. Artillery carbines.
Slide, sight, rifle, M.-H., Mark II	Interchangeable between Marks II and III., M.-H. rifles.
Slide, sight, rifle, M.-E., Mark I	Special.
Slide, sight, carbine, Cavalry, M.-H., Mark I	Interchangeable between Mark I, M.-H., Cavalry, and Marks I, II, and III, M.-H. Artillery carbines.
Slide, sight, carbine, Cavalry, M.-M., Mark I*	Interchangeable between Marks I* and II,* M.-M., Cavalry, carbines.
Slide, sight, carbine, Cavalry, M.-M., Mark III	Interchangeable between Mark III, M.-M., Cavalry, and Marks II and III, M.-M. Artillery carbines.
Slide, sight, match-shooting rifle, M.-E., Mark I	Special.
Spring, sight, back, rifle, M.-H., Mark II	,,
Spring, sight, back, rifle, M.-H., Mark III	Interchangeable between Mark III, M.-H., and Mark I, M.-E. rifles ; also Mark III, M.-M., Cavalry, and Marks II and III, M.-M. Artillery carbines.
Spring, sight, back, carbine, M.-H.	Interchangeable between Mark I, M.-H., Cavalry, Marks I, II, and III, M.-H. Artillery ; also Marks I* and II,* M-M. Cavalry carbines.
Leaves, sight, back, rifle, M.-H., Mark II	Interchangeable between Marks II and III, M.-H. rifles.
Leaves, sight, back, rifle, M.-E., Mark I	Special.
Leaves, sight, back, carbine, Cavalry, M.-H., Mark I	Interchangeable between Mark I M.-H., Cavalry, and Marks I, II, and III, M.-H., Artillery carbines.

Nomenclature of Parts.	
Leaves, sight, back, carbine, Cavalry, M.-M., Mark I*	Interchangeable between Marks I* and II*, M.-M., carbines, Cavalry
Leaves, sight, back, carbine, Cavalry, M.-M., Mark III	Interchangeable between Mark III, M.-M., Cavalry, and Marks II and III, M.-M. Artillery carbines.
Pin, sight, axis, rifle, M.-H., Mark II	Interchangeable between Marks II and III, M.-H., and Mark I, M.-E. rifles, Mark III, M.-M., Cavalry, and Marks II and III, M.-M. Artillery carbines.
Pin, sight, axis, carbine, Cavalry, M.-H., Mark I	Interchangeable between Mark I, M.-H., Cavalry, Marks I, II, III, M.-H. Artillery; also Marks I* and II*, M.-M., Cavalry, carbines
Screw, sight, spring, rifle, M.-H., Mark II	Interchangeable between all rifles and carbines except Mark I, M.-H., Cavalry, and Mark I and III, M.-H., Artillery carbines.
Screw, sight, bed, rifle, M.-H., Mark II	Interchangeable between all rifles and carbines except Mark I, M.-H., Cavalry, and Marks I and III, M.-H. Artillery carbines.
Screw, sight, bed, and spring, carbine, Cavalry, M.-H., Mark I (2)	Interchangeable between Mark I, M.-H., Cavalry, and Marks I and III, M.-H. Artillery carbines.
Stop, barrel-stud, rifle, M.-H., Mark II	Interchangeable between Mark II, M.-H., rifle; and Mark II, M.-H., Artillery carbine.
Stop, barrel-stud, carbine, Cavalry, M.-M., Mark III	Interchangeable between Mark III, M.-M., Cavalry, and Mark II, M.-M. Artillery carbines.
Stop-nut, rifle, M.-H., Mark II	Interchangeable between Mark II, M.-H. rifle, and Mark II, M.-H. Artillery carbines.
Stop-nut, rifle, M.-H., Mark III	Interchangeable between Mark III, M.-H., and Mark I, M.E., rifles; also Mark I, M.-H., Cavalry, and Marks I and III, M.-H. Artillery carbines.
Stop-nut, rifle, M.-M. ·303″	Interchangeable between all M.-M. ·303-inch arms.
Striker, rifle, M.-H., Mark II	Interchangeable between Mark II, M.-H. rifle, and Mark II, M.-H. Artillery carbine.
Striker, rifle, M.-H., Mark III	Interchangeable between Mark III, M.-H. rifle; also Mark I, M.-H. Cavalry, and Marks I and III, M.-H. Artillery carbines.
Striker, rifle, M.-M. ·303″	Interchangeable between all M.-M. ·303-inch arms, and Mark I, M.-E. rifle.

Nomenclature of Parts.	
Swivel, butt	Interchangeable between Artillery carbines and rifles of Rifle Regiments; also Mounted Infantry, and Mark I, M.-E. rifle.
Swivel, guard, rifle, M.-H., Mark II	Interchangeable between Marks II and III, M.-H. rifles.
Swivel, band, upper, rifle, M.-H., Mark II	Interchangeable between Marks II and III, M.-H., rifles; also Marks I, II and III, M.-H., Artillery, and Marks II and III, M.-M., Artillery carbines.
Swivel, band, lower, rifle, M.-E., Mark I	Special.
Swivel, piling, rifle, M.-E,, Mark I	,,
Trigger rifle M.E., Mark I	,,
Trigger, rifle M.-H., Mark II.	Interchangeable between all arms, except rifle, M.-E., Mark I.
,, screw	Interchangeable between all arms.
,, spring	,. ,, ,,
,, ,, screw	,, ,, ,,
Tumbler	,. ,, ,,
	,, ,, ,,

II.—DIRECTIONS FOR CLEANING M.-H., M.-M., AND M.-E. ARMS.

N.B.—The oil used should be Rangoon in the case of M.-H. arms, and rifle oil in the case of ·303″ arms—the latter to be well shaken before use. All barrels will be wiped out before firing, and thoroughly cleaned and oiled with the oil specified after firing, and again thoroughly cleaned and oiled as soon after parade as possible. Too much care cannot be bestowed in keeping the inside of the barrels perfectly clean and uninjured. In wet weather the arms will invariably be cleaned immediately after the men return to their quarters.

1. All the parts connected with the breech-action must be kept perfectly clean.

2. Rangoon oil only to be used for this purpose; the use of hard or cutting substances, such as emery, brick dust, sand paper, &c., being strictly forbidden.

3. Care must be taken not to injure the face of the block in cleaning, especially the striker hole.

4. The action can usually be sufficiently oiled by pouring a few drops of oil through the opening, between the lever and body, when the end of the lever loop is drawn out of its catch-block, and the rifle held with the trigger-guard uppermost.

5. Open the breech by depressing the lever.

6. M.-H. Arms—Wrap a piece of damp rag, flannel, or tow, round the jag of the cleaning rod, so as to cover it, and rub carefully up and down the barrel to remove the fouling. Water should not be used. If the cleaning-rod sticks fast in the barrel, it should be driven back by blows with a wooden mallet, not dragged through the muzzle.

7. M.-H. Arms—Replace the piece of damp rag, &c., by a dry one, and then by an oiled one (woollen, if possible), and pass it a few times up and down the barrel.

8. To clean the bore of ·303-inch arms daily, and also after using cordite ammunition.

Oil the gauze of the pull-through well with rifle oil, drop the weight through the barrel from the breech and pull the gauze completely through. Then insert in the loop nearest the gauze a piece of dry flannelette, 4 inches by 2 inches, and draw it through the barrel as before; the flannelette should never be pulled back when partly through, as it would probably jam. A second piece of flannelette may be required to make the barrel perfectly clean. Finally an oiled piece of flannelette should be drawn through.

When the gauze on the pull-through, in consequence of frequent use, ceases to fit the barrel tightly, narrow strips of flannelette or paper may be inserted under each side, to increase its diameter. No larger piece of flannelette than 4 inches by 2 inches should be used, and it may sometimes be reduced in width with advantage.

When all signs of fouling are removed from the bore, it should be left oily, and not wiped out with a clean rag.

Water should on no account be used after firing with cordite ammunition.

It saves time if two men assist one another, one at each end of the pull-through. After firing with cordite ammunition, the bore should be cleaned out at once, and not left uncleaned.

9. Wipe the breech-end of the barrel, the interior of the body, and the breech block, as well as possible with an oiled rag.

10. Ease springs and press the end of the lever into the catch-block.

III.—DIRECTIONS WITH REGARD TO THE PERIODICAL INSPECTION OF M.-H., M.-M., AND M.-E. ARMS BY SERJEANT-INSTRUCTORS.

Militia.

1. The Serjeant-Instructor is thoroughly to look over the arms after the training, and also from time to time between the visits of the Armourer-Serjeant, with a view of ascertaining their condition.

2. He is not to strip the action unless there is reason to suppose that it is rusty inside, or clogged with oil or dirt, or in order to replace a component. (*See* Section IX.)

3. He is not to strip the arm generally, unless to replace a component. As a rule the fore-end should not be taken off the barrel unless there is reason to suppose the latter is rusty underneath ; but after much exposure to wet weather at drill, or in camp, the fore-ends should be removed. Before re-assembling the barrels and fore-ends should be well oiled.

Volunteers.

4. The Serjeant-Instructor will carefully examine the whole of the arms at least once in three months, to ascertain their condition.

5. He is not to strip the action unless there is reason to suppose that it is rusty inside, or clogged with oil or dirt, or in order to replace a component. (*See* Section IX.)

6. He is not to strip the arm generally, unless to replace a component. As a rule the fore-end should not be taken off the barrel unless there is reason to suppose the latter is rusty underneath ; but after much exposure to wet weather at drill, or in camp, the fore-ends should be removed. Before re-assembling, the barrels and fore-ends should be well oiled.

7. Should the action require a new component, other than those mentioned on page 21, the arm should be sent to the Inspector of Small-Arms, Royal Small-Arms Factory, Birmingham.

IV.—DIRECTIONS FOR STRIPPING AND ASSEMBLING THE ARM AND ACTION.

1. The following directions are issued as a guide to the Serjeant-Instructors (or N.C.O. detailed for the duty), should it be found necessary to perform the operations referred to in Section III. ; but it is to be understood that the more rarely the arm is stripped the better.

STRIPPING THE ARM.

2. The arm to be stripped should be carefully and securely held in the vice in the manner shown at the Royal Small-Arms Factory, and the Serjeant-Instructors (or N.C.O. detailed for the duty), are particularly cautioned against putting the gun in the vice without its being properly protected by wood clams lined with cork.

STRIPPING THE ACTION.

Rifles, M-H. and M.-E., and Carbines M.-H. and M.-M.

1. Close the breech.

2. Knock out the block axis-pin by placing a drift on the slit-head of the pin, first removing any dirt there may be in the slit.

3. Depress the lever and hold down the front end of the block with the left thumb, close the lever, and the block will spring out.

4. Take out the block, turn the curve in the head of the keeper-screw fair with the curve in the stop-nut, unscrew the stop-nut ; the striker and mainspring will then fall out.

5. Turn the curve in the head of the screw-keeper of the indicator fair with axis hole, press out the axis-pin, and take out the tumbler.

6. Turn out the extractor axis-screw, and remove the extractor, trigger-guard, and lever.

N.B.—The trigger and spring should not be stripped.

STRIPPING THE FURNITURE, BARREL, AND STOCK.

Rifles, M.-H. and M.-E.

1. Draw the cleaning-rod in M.-H., first turning the rod so that the cam is against the rod-holder, unscrew clearing-rod to the left in M.-E. The rod will then draw straight out. In no case is the rod-head to be pulled with any force away from the barrel.

2. Remove the upper band stop-pin.

3. Remove the barrel stud-pin in M.-H., Mark II.

4. Partly unturn the band screws, and take off the bands. The lower band stop-pin should not be removed.

5. Pull off the stock fore-end from the muzzle of the barrel, and the hook will disengage from the end of the body (Mark III), M.-H., and Mark I, M.-E.

6. Drive the stock fore-end off the barrel stud at the breech-end with the wood drift (Mark II), M.-H.

7. Take off the butt-plate.

8. Turn out the stock-bolt, and take off the stock butt.

Carbines, Artillery and Cavalry, M.-H. and M.-M., Stripping.

1. Draw the
- cleaning rod, M.-H. — In Marks II and III, Artillery M.-H., first turning the rod so that the cam is against the rod holder.
- clearing-rod, M.-M. — In Marks I* and II*, Cavalry, M.-M., the rod unscrews to the right. In Mark III, Cavalry, M.-M., and Marks II and III, Artillery, M.-M., the rod unscrews to the left.

2. Remove the upper band
- In Mark I, Cavalry M.-H., and Marks I* and II*, Cavalry M.-M., remove the upper band screw, and take off the band.
- In Mark I, Artillery M.-H., partly unturn the upper band screw, and take off the band.
- In Marks II and III, Artillery M.-H., remove upper band stop-pin, and partly unturn upper band screw, and take off band.
- In Mark III, Cavalry M.-M., and Marks II and III, Artillery M.-M. (the upper band is combined with nose-cap), take out nose-cap screw, drive nose-cap off fore-end, and turn so that the foresight can pass through slot in nose-cap.

3. Remove the barrel stud-pin
- In Mark II, Artillery M.-H., Mark III, Cavalry M.-M., and Mark II, Artillery M.-M.

4. Remove the lower band
- In Mark I, Cavalry M.-H., Marks I* and II*, Cavalry M.-M., Mark I, Artillery M.-H., unscrew the lower band as far as the screw will allow, land the front side on the edge of stock shoulder, push open the opposite side with screw-driver in the slit of the screw, and press the band over the stock shoulder, and take off the band.
- In Marks II and III, Artillery M.-H., as directed at 4 in above for rifle.
- The Mark III, Cavalry M.-M., and Marks II and III, Artillery M.-M., have no lower bands.

5. Remove the stock fore-end
- In Mark I, Cavalry M.-H., Marks I* and II*, Cavalry M.-M., Marks I and III, Artillery M.-H., and Mark III, Artillery M.-M., pull off the stock fore-end from the muzzle of the barrel, and the hook will disengage from the end of the body.
- In Mark II, Artillery M.-H., Mark III, Cavalry M.-M., and Mark II, Artillery M.-M., drive the stock fore-end off the barrel stud at the breech end with the wood drift.

6 and 7. For carbines as directed at 7 and 8 in above for rifle.

ASSEMBLING THE ACTION, BARREL, STOCK, AND FURNITURE.

Rifles, M.-H. and M.-E.

1. Replace the stock butt, observing that the stock-bolt washer is in its place in the stock butt, and screw up the stock-bolt.

2. Screw on the butt-plate.

3. Place the hook fore-end in the body, so as to engage inside the recess, pressing the fore-end up the barrel at muzzle (Mark III), M.-H., and Mark I, M.-E.

4. Slide the stock fore-end on the barrel stud (Mark II), M.-H.

5. Replace the bands and turn home the band screws.

6. Replace the upper band stop-pin.

7. Replace the barrel stud-pin (Mark II), M.-H.

8. Replace the cleaning-rod in M.-H.—clearing rod in M.-E. When the rod is in its proper position, the cam is away from the rod-holder, and the head of the rod-holder in the groove in M.-H., screw in to right in M.-E.

9. Place the lever and tumbler in the trigger-guard, slide the guard with the lever and tumbler into the body, and replace the axis-pin with the indicator pointing upwards in the direction of the block axis-pin, and screw round the head of the keeper-screw to its proper bedding.

10. Replace the extractor and turn in the axis-screw.

11. Place the striker in the block, and drop in the mainspring, screw home the stop-nut, and turn the head of the keeper-screw into its bedding.

12. Turn the striker round until the longer opening of the slot is downwards.

13. Place the block in the body with the front end lowest; hold the lever with the right hand, the thumb pressing the indicator forward, the trigger being pressed back by the forefinger; press hard on the knuckle of block with the heel of the left hand to force it into its seat; at the same time depress and work the lever to get the crane of the tumbler into the slot in the striker.

14. Compress the sides of the block axis-pin with the pliers about a quarter of an inch from the divided end, preparatory to placing it in the body. Place it in the body.

Assembling Carbines M.-H. and M.-M.

1 and 2. As directed above for rifle.

3. Same as directed above for rifle, in carbines Mark 1, Cavalry M.-H., Marks I* and II*, Cavalry M.-M., Marks I and III, Artillery M.-H. and Mark III, Artillery M.M.

4. Same as directed above for rifle, in carbines Mark II, Artillery M.-H., Mark III, Cavalry M.-M., and Mark II. Artillery M.-M.

5. Replace bands, upper and lower, and turn home screws in all arms except Mark III, Cavalry M.-M., and Marks II and III, Artillery M.-M., in these carbines replace nose-cap, and turn home screw.

6. Replace the upper band stop-pin in carbines, Marks II and III, Artillery M.-H.

7. Replace the barrel stud-pin in carbines, Mark II, Artillery M.-H., Mark III, Cavalry M.-M., and Mark II, Artillery M.-M.

8. Replace the cleaning-rod in M.-H.—clearing rod in M.M.

9, 10, 11, 12, 13, and 14. As directed above for rifle.

V.—Examination of Strikers.

For this purpose a service cartridge will be prepared as follows:—

Remove the bullet, wad, &c., from a service cartridge, and shake out the powder. Place the empty case in the chamber and explode the cap. File the empty case through at $1\frac{1}{4}$ inches from the base disc, taking care not to deform the case. Place inside the empty case, so prepared, a small cylinder of wood, in order to prevent it becoming dented, and fasten it in the case by punching two or three small holes round the edge. Fill the indentation in the exploded cap with soap, level with the base disc.

To test the condition of the point of the striker:—Load the arm with the dummy cartridge, and fire. On withdrawing the cartridge an impression of the point of the striker will be found in the soap should the striker be perfect. Should the striker make no impression in the soap when the arm is fired, the point of the striker must be broken, and a new striker should be inserted.

VI.—Easing Springs.

The breech being open, place the thumb on the thumb-seat, the forefinger on the trigger, and the remaining fingers under the guard, press the trigger firmly without touching the lever, and when the lever is closed, secure it in the catch-block by clasping the bow of the lever and small of the butt with the right hand.

N.B.—Springs must never be eased when a cartridge is in the chamber.

VII.—INSTRUCTIONS FOR REPLACING, IN THE FIELD, MAINSPRINGS AND STRIKERS OF MARTINI-HENRY, MARTINI-METFORD, AND MARTINI-ENFIELD CARBINES AND RIFLES.

1. The following instructions for replacing, in the field, strikers and mainsprings of Martini-Henry, Martini-Metford, and Martini-Enfield carbines and rifles, using for the purpose the bayonet, sword-bayonet, or sword, and the implement action, will be strictly adhered to.

For the Rifles.

2. Place the muzzle on the ground, and the butt underneath the right arm. With the drift of the implement knock out the block axis-pin by striking the top of the former with the inside flat face of the bayonet blade, between the end of the groove and the socket.

For the Carbines.

3. Place the muzzle on the ground and lean on the butt. With the drift of the implement knock out the block axis-pin by striking the top of the former with the pommel of the sword or sword-bayonet, using the spring side in the latter case.

For Rifles and Carbines.

4. Take out the block, and with the small screw-driver turn the curve in the head of the keeper-screw fair with the curve in the stop-nut. With the stop-nut screw-driver take out the stop-nut. Renew the striker or mainspring, and re-assemble the block.

5. Place the assembled block in the body, and with the hook and jaw of the implement compress the sides of the block axis-pin at about a quarter of an inch from the divided end, insert the pin in the axis hole, and drive it home with the head of the implement.

6. Examine the muzzle of the barrel to see that it is free from dirt, &c.

VIII.—INSTRUCTIONS FOR USING TRIGGER-TESTERS.

Rifles and Carbines.

1. The "pull off" of military small-arms is regulated so as to require a mean weight of about 7 lb. to be applied to the finger-piece of the trigger, in order to release the trigger-nose from the bent in the tumbler : this result is obtained only when the components of the action, including the trigger, are perfectly clean, and free from dried-up oil, or other matter causing obstruction to the free working of the various parts.

In order, therefore, to obtain trustworthy indications of the weight of the "pull off" the Serjeant-Instructor will thoroughly examine the actions of the arms which are to be tested, and clean and oil such as he finds require to be so treated, especial attention being paid to the following points—viz., that the block does not jam against the breech-end of the barrel when it is being closed, and that the trigger-screw is screwed well home.

2. In weighing the "pull off," the arm should be rigidly fixed in the vice in a horizontal position, the indicator side uppermost. The trigger-tester should be held in a line diagonally across the grip, and immediately over the lower corner of the body.

3. Under no circumstance should the "pull off" be interfered with, but if it is found to be under 6 lb. or over 8 lb. the arm should be sent to the Chief Inspector of Small-Arms, Royal Small-Arms Factory, Birmingham.

IX.—Units of Militia, Artillery, and Infantry having a qualified Serjeant-Instructor with a certificate from the Chief Inspector of Small-Arms will be granted an annual allowance of spare parts in the following scale. The proportion will be kept up by annual demand on the Senior Ordnance Store Officer of the District (except in the Woolwich district, where the requisition will be sent to the Senior Ordnance Store Officer, Weedon) for such parts as may have been expended in repair during the previous year.

	For each Unit per 1,000 Arms.*
Pins, axis, block	2
,, ,, extractor	1
,, band, stop, upper‡	1
,, barrel, stud‡	1
Screws, keeper, indicator	3
,, ,, stop-nut	2
,, butt, plate	1
,, swivel, trigger guard‡	2
Springs, main { M.-H.	5
{ M.-M.	5
Strikers, { Mark II	25
{ ,, III	10
{ M.-M.	10
§Bayonets, { rings, locking, M.-H.	—
{ ,, ,, M.-E.	—
{ screws	—
§Sword-bayonets, screws, spring	—

* For other establishments a proportionate allowance will be supplied: fractional results in working out the proportion may be taken as whole numbers, and allowance is to be made for any numbers in possession of the corps.

‡ See table of parts for pattern of Arms having these components.

§ For those arms carrying bayonets or sword-bayonets of a pattern requiring these components.

X.—The following proportions of components of Martini-Henry, Martini-Metford, and Martini-Enfield arms will be issued to Volunteers and Yeomany to enable the Serjeant-Instructors to execute repairs.

Martini-Henry, Martini-Metford and Martini-Enfield Arms.	Annual proportion per 1,000 Arms.*
Pins, axis, block	5
,, extractor	3
,, stop, band, upper‡	3
,, stud, barrel‡	3
Screws, keeper, indicator	10
,, ,, stop-nut	10
,, swivel, trigger guard‡	10
Springs, main { M.-H.	10
{ M.-M.	10
Strikers { Mark II	45
{ ,, III	15
{ M.-M.	15
§Bayonets, { rings, locking M.-H.	3
{ ,, ,, M.-E.	3
{ screws	10
§Sword-bayonets, screws, spring	3
§Scabbards, sword-bayonets, screws, M.-H., carbine, Mark II	5

XI.—The following proportions of tools are supplied by the Ordnance Store Department for the use of the Serjeant-Instructor in repairing arms.

Braces, armourers'†	1
Bits, screw-driver, butt, plate, screw	1
,, ,, ,, stock-bolt	1
,, ,, ,, stop-nut	1
Clams, armourers', vice, pairs†	1
Corks, clam	2

* For other establishments a proportionate allowance will be supplied: fractional results in working out the proportion may be taken as whole numbers, and allowance is to be made for any numbers in possession of the corps. Some of the items being special to certain arms (*vide* details in Vocabulary) should only be demanded for those arms.

† These tools being common to armourers and other artificers should be demanded from the Commissary-General of Ordnance, under Woolwich Store Charge, No. 7.

‡ See table of parts for pattern of arms having these components.

§ For those arms carrying bayonets or sword-bayonets of a pattern requiring these components.

Drifts, fore-end, M.-H.	1*
,, wire, large	1
Drivers, screw, armourers', medium	1
,, ,, ,, small	1
Hammers, rivetting, 4 oz.†	1
Horses, armourers', with screws	2
Implements, action	1
Pliers, flatnose, pairs	1
Rods, armourers', cleaning, M.-H., (carbine or rifle as the case may be), or R.M.L.M. for .303″ arms	1
Testers, trigger, pull, M.-H.	1
Vices, standing, 36 lbs.§	1

* For Mark II M.-H. rifle and carbines Artillery M.-H., and M.-M. Mark II, and Cavalry M.-M. Mark III.

† These tools being common to armourers and other artificers should be demanded from the Commissary-General of Ordnance, under Woolwich Store Charge, No. 7.

§ These tools being common to armourers and other artificers, should be demanded from the Commissary-General of Ordnance, under Woolwich Store Charge, No. 8.

LONDON:

PRINTED FOR HER MAJESTY'S STATIONERY OFFICE,
BY HARRISON AND SONS,
PRINTERS IN ORDINARY TO HER MAJESTY.
[Wt. 25991 400 3 | 96—H & S 2625]

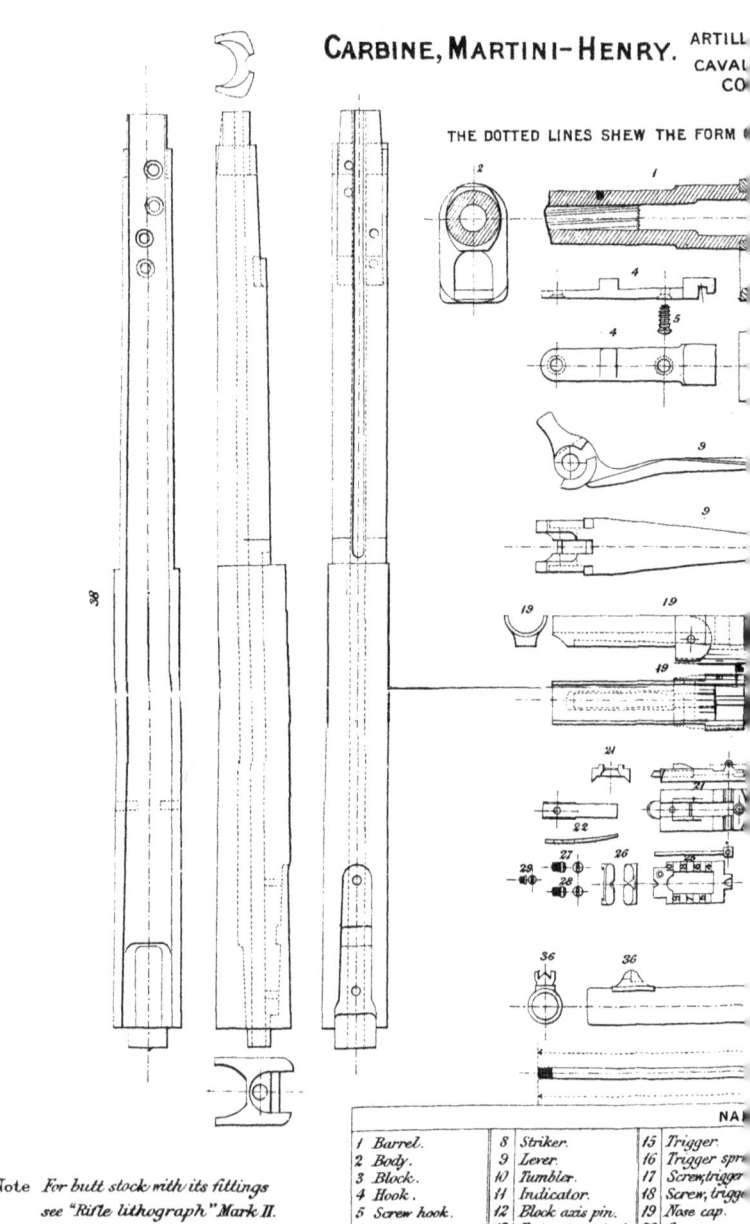

CARBINE, MARTINI-HENRY. ARTILL CAVAL CO

THE DOTTED LINES SHEW THE FORM

Note For butt stock with its fittings
see "Rifle lithograph" Mark II.

1	Barrel.	8	Striker.	15	Trigger.
2	Body.	9	Lever.	16	Trigger spri
3	Block.	10	Tumbler.	17	Screw, trigger
4	Hook.	11	Indicator.	18	Screw, trigge
5	Screw hook.	12	Block axis pin.	19	Nose cap.
6	Stop nut.	13	Extractor axis pin.	20	Screw, nose
7	Main spring.	14	Guard, trigger.	21	Sight bed.

Plate I.

MARK I (Approved 21.7.79 $\frac{7669}{4346}$ Paragraph 3615 list of Changes.)
„ 24.9 77 $\frac{7669}{4054}$ „ 3215 „ „ „

R. S. A. F.
569.

ONENT PARTS.
Half Size.

COMPONENTS SPECIAL TO THE ARTILLERY CARBINE.

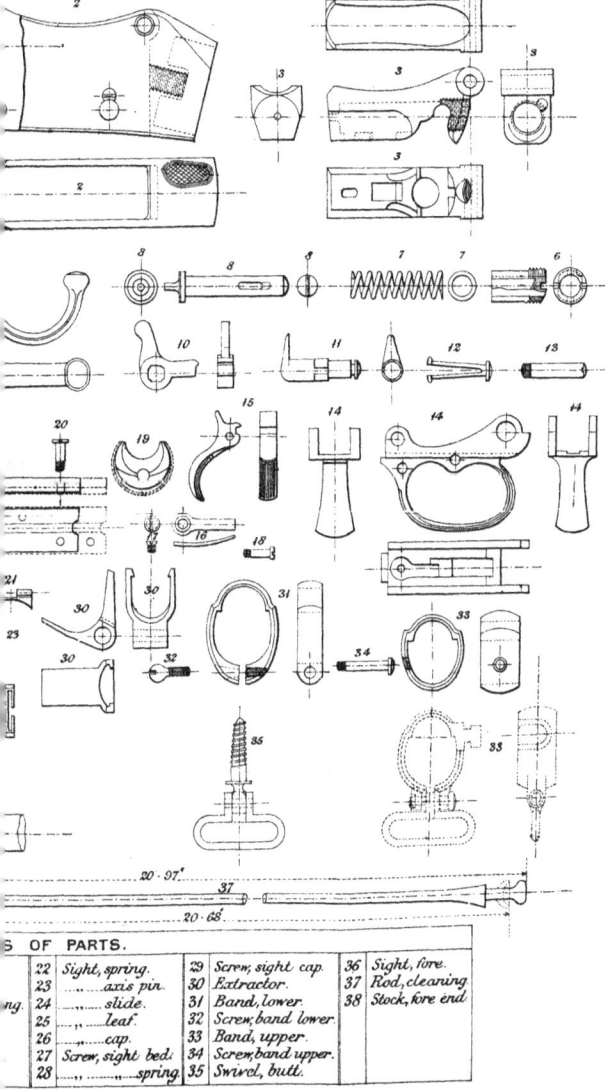

OF PARTS.

22	Sight, spring.	29	Screw, sight cap.	36	Sight, fore.
23	„ axis pin.	30	Extractor.	37	Rod, cleaning.
24	„ slide.	31	Band, lower.	38	Stock, fore end.
25	„ leaf.	32	Screw, band lower.		
26	„ cap.	33	Band, upper.		
27	Screw, sight bed.	34	Screw, band upper.		
28	„ „ spring.	35	Swivel, butt.		

Wyman & Sons, L^{td} Lith 7204 5 95

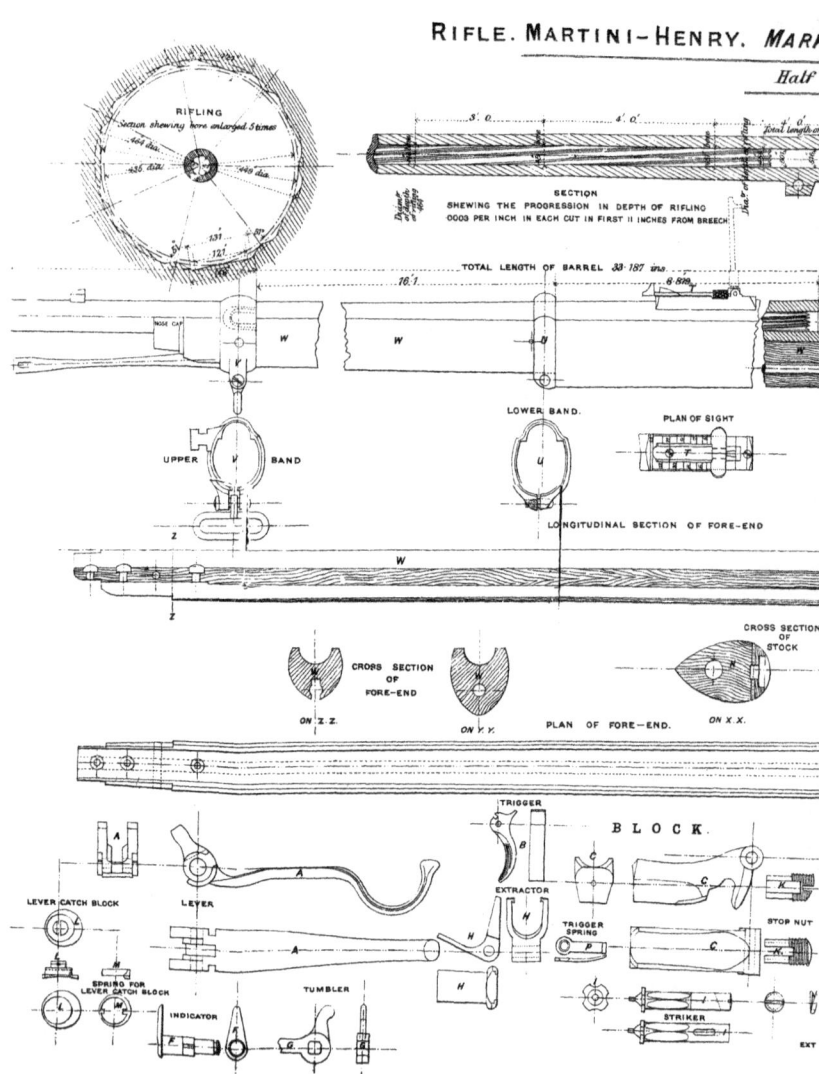

// (§ 3193 LIST OF CHANGES.) Plate II.

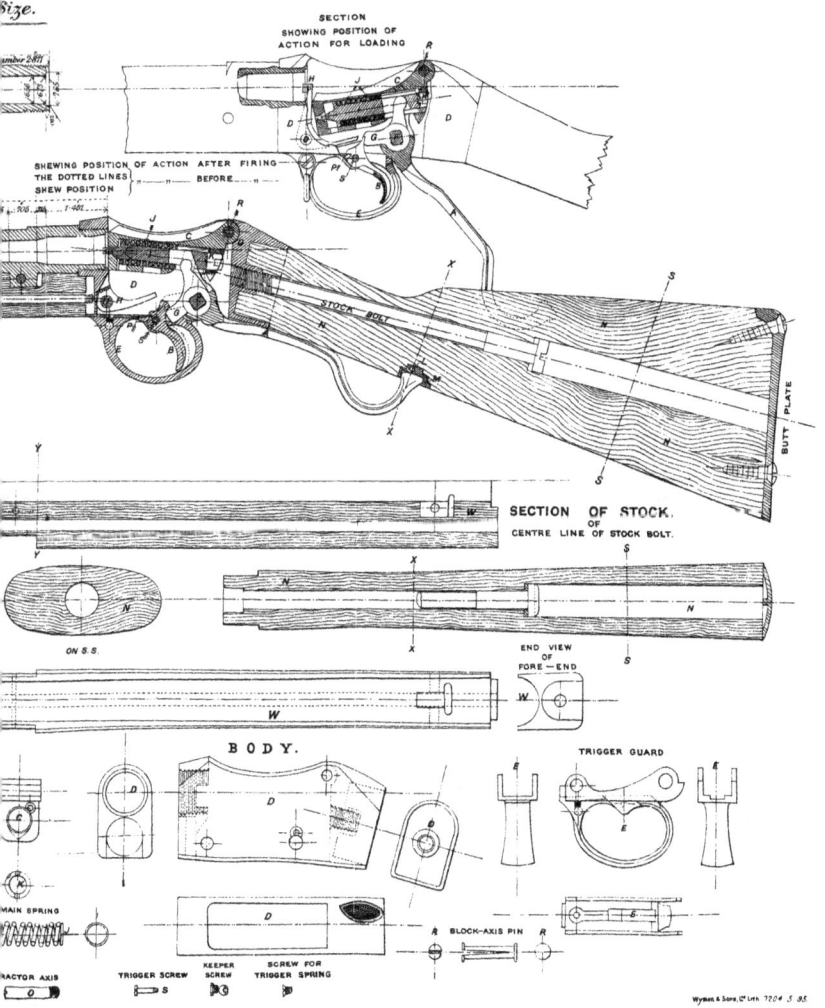

RIFLE.
COMPONENTS

BARREL

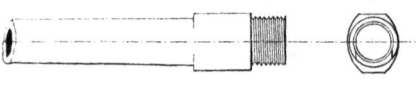

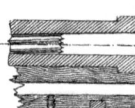

CLEANING ROD.

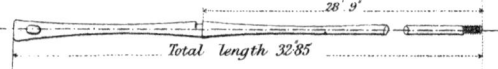

HOOK

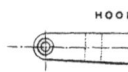

LONGITUDINAL SECTION OF FORE

PLAN OF FORE-END.

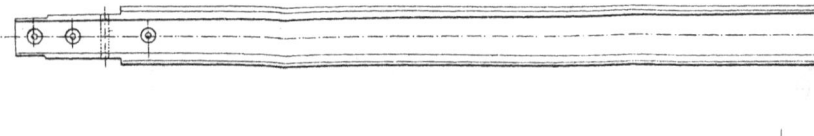

INDICATOR.   STRIKER.

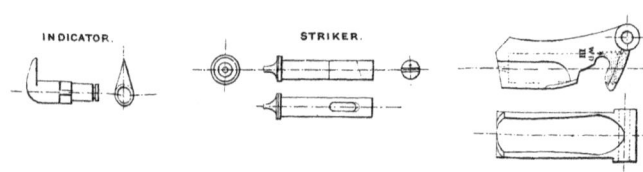

ARTINI-HENRY.
PECIAL TO MARK III.

Half Size.

R.S.A.F.
783

Plate III.

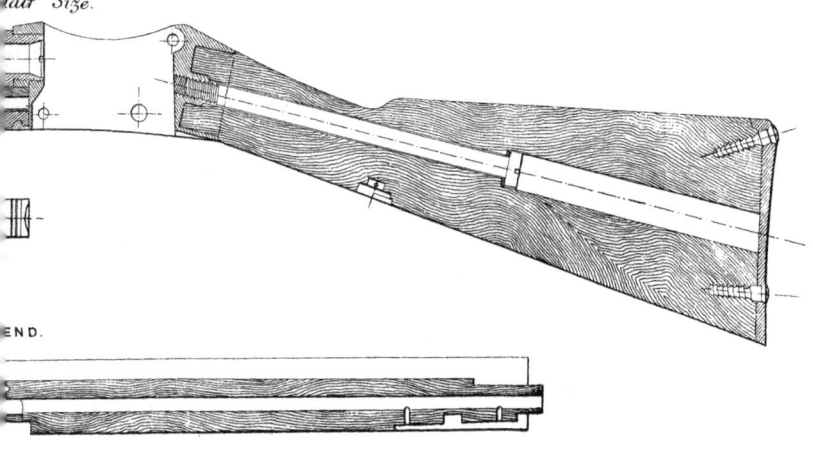

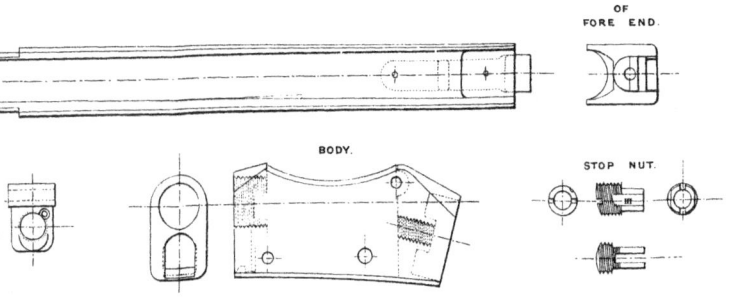

END VIEW
OF
FORE END.

BODY.

STOP NUT.

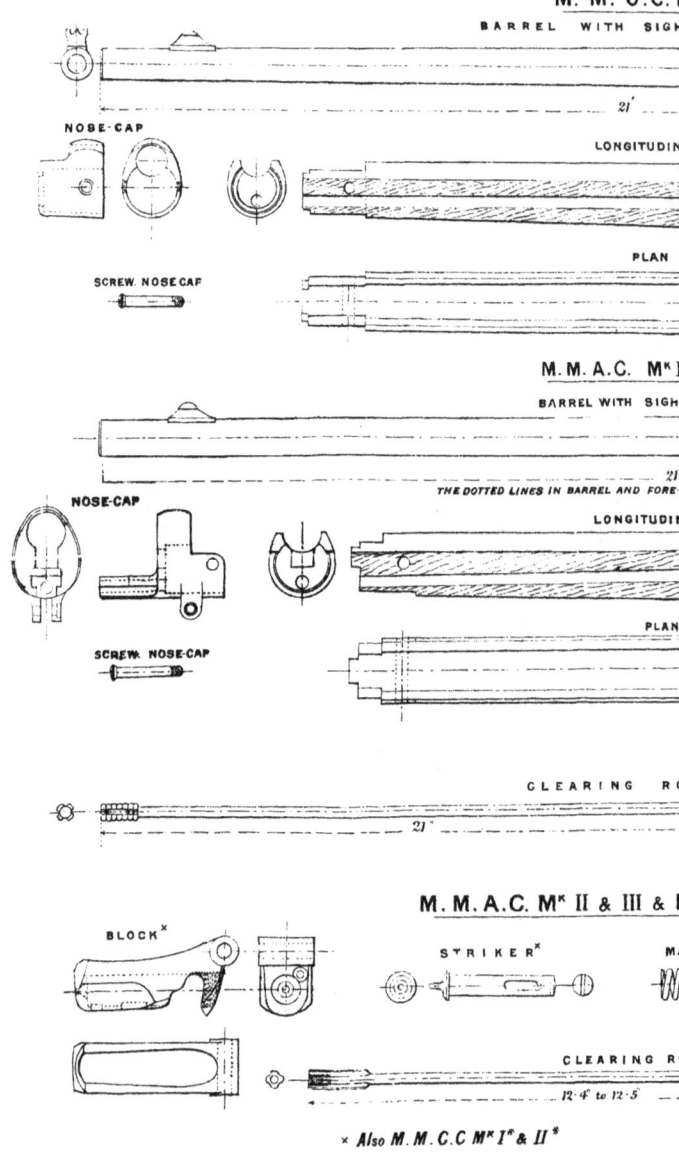

Plate IV. A.I.D. 92

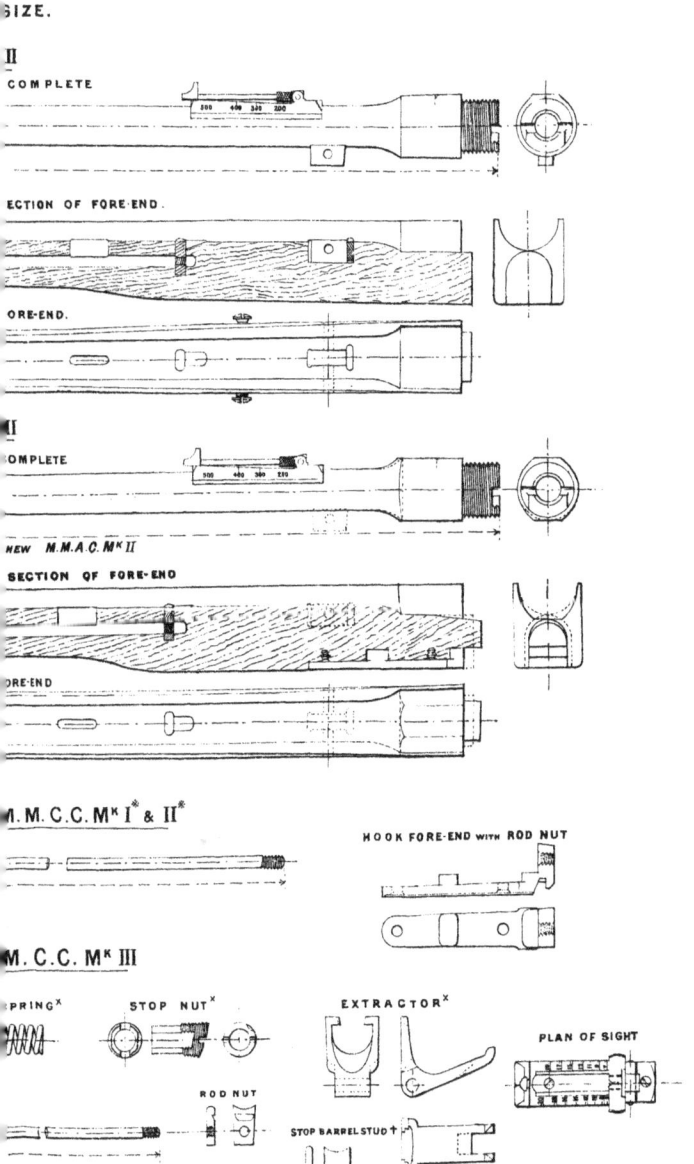

www.ingramcontent.com/pod-product-compliance
Lightning Source LLC
Chambersburg PA
CBHW031437040426
42444CB00006B/854